The Student

Sarah Cockings, from Whitley Bay, near Newcastle, was a 21-year-old student living with her parents when she won £3,405,705 in April 2005. She quit her studies and now lives in a luxury five-bedroom home.

Winning the lottery is one of the most amazing and strange things that can happen to you. One moment I was a student wondering if I could afford to buy a sandwich for lunch, and the next I had more money than I could dream of. More money than my parents and my entire family had put together. I couldn't believe it. Little me, a millionaire!

That's how I came to be sitting on a Turkish beach sipping a cocktail under a blazing sun, instead of walking along the wet and windy front at Whitley Bay with a cup of tea. Just a few months earlier I would never even have picked up a brochure for a resort like this because I was so broke.

I was just another struggling student, taking packed lunches into university to save money for the odd night out or to buy something nice to wear from a regular high street store. Now, there was luxury everywhere. Waiters to bring me drinks, a wonderful pool to cool off in, and five-star restaurants where I didn't really have to look at the bill.

But every now and then my mind would flash back to the moment I won. The moment I was transformed from a student to a millionaire. The moment that changed my life.

You can't prepare or practise to be a lottery winner. It just hits you head on and you have to deal with it. The win changes everything and, in a sense, you can never be the same again.

When I won, I was studying to be a social worker and had just completed my first year at the university. I was living at home with my mum and dad in Whitley Bay, near Newcastle. We are a close family and I get on brilliantly with my sisters Emma, who is 18 months older, and Alex, who is three years younger.

I had no real worries that I can remember, but money was tight. I had a student loan that gave me around £800 every three months, but it didn't go far. I had a boyfriend of three years,

Roy, who was an engineer and a really nice bloke. A DVD and a Chinese were about as exciting as it got, but I never felt I was missing something.

I was very happy. My biggest concern was all the studying and whether I'd get the marks to graduate.

I was just like most girls, I suppose. I've always been a really ordinary girl. From the age of four I've been obsessed with babies, prams and dolls. My mum always said that I just wanted to be a mum and be married.

It's not that I didn't have ambition. I wanted to do the best I could and make something of myself. I would be happy with a decent job and a family; it's what I had planned. But then the lottery jackpot came from nowhere.

Even if they're happy, everyone has moments when they dream of winning the lottery. Those times when you do that mental checklist of what you are going to buy with your millions. But you never think in a million years that you are really going to win. It's all just daydreaming.

I played the lottery every now and again. The only time I gave winning much thought was when I needed a little car to get me to university. I would definitely buy a Mini Cooper, a really nice one, if I was lucky enough to win one day.

Then I'd stop dreaming. But it was this dream of a car that changed my life.

My parents said they would loan me £2,000 to buy a Nissan Micra. After shopping around for the car, I called in at the Whitley Lodge Post Office with Roy. My mum worked for the post office side there and Alex worked behind the sweet counter.

I decided to have a go at the lottery and suddenly had a strong feeling, a sort of premonition about winning. I picked three lines. On the second, Roy bumped my arm. I was going to get rid of the ticket and do another one, but something stopped me. I stuck with the completely random numbers I chose.

It was amazing because I didn't know why I'd picked them and wouldn't have picked them again. I went to the counter, Alex put the ticket on, and off we went.

I normally just bought the ticket and forgot about it. This time something played on my mind, even though I'm not a superstitious type of person. It was a spooky feeling.

That night, I watched Sweet Sixteen, the TV

programme about girls with millionaire parents who get everything they want. I remember saying, 'How lucky are they?' They all get amazing cars for their birthdays. At that moment, the draw was probably being made.

We watched a film and Roy went home around 11 p.m. I kissed Mum and Dad goodnight then went on my laptop to check the cost of insurance for the Micra. Roy texted me goodnight and reminded me to check my lottery ticket online. I got the ticket and smoothed it out because it was all crumpled. Then I went through the numbers.

Never for a moment did I think I'd win anything. I only checked the numbers because Roy had reminded me and I was still awake.

Sitting on my bed, I was really chuffed when I found out I'd won a tenner. I thought that would be where it ended. Nice to get a tenner, put it towards a new top but nothing more.

I then looked at the other numbers and they were all mine. I was scared to death to look at them again. There was no way, was there?

My heart was racing and my mouth was getting dry as I checked again and again. There were three or four games drawn every Saturday night so I could easily have made a mistake. That would have been typical. I could have been lucky with the Thunderball numbers rather than the main draw.

I just thought, 'Nah, it's impossible, totally impossible.' I could think of more reasons why I hadn't won rather than believing the proof in front of my eyes. I was just an ordinary girl who had gone to Whitley Bay High School. I couldn't have won, could I?

It got very confusing, very fast. It felt like the world was flashing before me and the room was spinning. It was a very strange sensation.

I remember running downstairs where my dad was sitting reading a book. He's a really calm person, and he could see there was something wrong.

'Dad, I think I've won the national lottery,' I blurted out.

He started to check as I hopped about. I couldn't believe it, but if my dad said I'd won, then that was it. He confirmed it. I yelled 'Wooo' and ran upstairs to tell my mum.

I woke her up and stammered, 'I think I've won the lottery.' She went right back to sleep. It was like a comedy sketch because after a few seconds she woke up again and asked, 'Did someone say they'd won the lottery?'

Then it all began. It was a hysterical, mad feeling. But in a good way. I was shaking and I wanted to burst out laughing. I couldn't keep still and felt waves of excitement and fear. I must have looked a bit of a sight racing around the house.

I remember holding on to the ticket, not knowing then quite how much I'd won. It was all a bit of a jumble and I thought I'd maybe won £80,000, an amazing amount. My dad went online to get the prize breakdown and it said three winners were sharing £9 million. I thought I must be the fourth winner, but he said, 'No, you're one of the three, pet.'

My dad hid the ticket in page 124 in a book in a cupboard. He wasn't taking any chances. It was weird because we started thinking all the local burglars were looking over our hedge. I was totally paranoid that everyone knew.

I couldn't wait to tell my sisters. Alex was working in a nightclub in Whitley Bay and Emma was there on a night out, so they came back together in a taxi at about 3 a.m. My parents and I looked really serious when they came through the door and we saw their faces drop. They both asked what was wrong, fearing bad news.

I shouted out, 'I've just won more than £3

million on the national lottery!' They started screaming and all hell broke loose.

They were booked in to have boob job consultations at a Manchester clinic the following Friday, so the first thing they said was, 'Oh my God, can we get our boobs done now?!'

We sat up till 5 a.m. when Mum made us go to sleep. She got me back up at 9 a.m. As soon as I woke up, I hoped I hadn't just had a really clear dream. Please say it's not a dream, please.

Thankfully, the ticket was still safe and the numbers hadn't changed overnight. We called Camelot who were able to confirm the win. That made me feel a lot calmer.

My dad kept hold of the ticket so I knew it was safe. I was on a work placement through my course so I went in and said I wouldn't be there on Wednesday. When they found out that I would be missing work to collect a winning cheque, they said, 'Why are you here now, you crazy woman?'

I was running on adrenalin. I don't think I ate for days but it kind of felt normal. I remember going to get an outfit for the Wednesday. I hardly had any money so I just went into regular shops. It was strange because I was worth £3 million, but I only had £30 to spend on a cardigan and top as I didn't have the cheque yet.

I was really calm when I got the money. I was still in shock. Everyone was amazed that I wasn't jumping up and down about it, but I think it was still sinking in.

The amount was so huge that it all seemed like Monopoly money. I couldn't picture what £3 million would look like in real bank notes. The money was put straight into a bank account for me so I would never know, but I couldn't resist going to the cash point machine to check my balance.

My heart stopped when the amount came up on the screen. All those numbers! Normally it would say about £15 max and now it showed millions. It was very weird to see those digits. I was a millionaire. It was incredible, amazing and really unbelievable! I still get shivers when I think of that moment. The thrill of being a winner never leaves you.

The first thing I bought was a watch, half price in a sale. It was £83 and I was dead chuffed. It seems odd that I didn't go out on an instant spending spree. But when you have been brought up to be careful with money, it doesn't come easily to start throwing money around.

We weren't going to go public but news of the win leaked out. Then it seemed pointless to hide it.

I was a bit nervous about people finding out. I was worried about what they might think, but it's been fine. People would say how I was so young and normal, and everyone was really, really happy for me.

At that point, I was planning on going back to university. But because I was only 21, there was a lot of publicity. I enjoyed the attention and the chance to sample a bit of the showbiz lifestyle. What girl wouldn't like that?

The offers of photographs and TV appearances came flooding in. I thought, why not? It was a golden opportunity, so I put my studies on hold. I was only going to be a young lottery winner for so long.

It was a big decision that changed my life. I did want to be a social worker and wasn't sure about leaving university early, but this chance had landed in my lap. I really enjoyed the photo shoots and the TV and didn't feel nervous at all about being interviewed. I did photo shoots with top photographers and have great memories and pictures to look back on when I'm a granny. I was on TV quite a few times and even did a documentary for American TV.

I'm into TV and celebrities, so it was fun. I got within touching distance of the singer Will Young and David Schwimmer from Friends. The actress Drew Barrymore was on GMTV at the same time as me, and I went to the Ant and Dec film premiere.

It was a fantastic whirlwind of attention, but behind the glamour there was still a life to lead. I think people expect you to be instantly and permanently happy after you win the lottery. You still have to get on with life though. It is no guarantee of happiness.

The hardest thing I had to do was split with Roy. The relationship had reached the end and we both knew it. But this is where being a lottery winner does change how people view you. A student splitting up with her boyfriend grabs no one's attention, but a lottery winner? That's totally different.

I was worried that people would think the money was to blame. Maybe they would judge me, thinking we'd split because I felt I was better than Roy or didn't need him now. But the truth was the relationship had run its course and we were more like brother and sister. There was no bad feeling from him, and his view was the only one I cared about.

It was hard to ignore the others though.

Newspapers wrote about the split and formed their own opinions without knowing the facts. That was tough for both of us to deal with.

Some people expect you to change. But I wasn't flashy, driving Ferraris or buying mansions, so they had nothing much to say about me.

I still do the same things and have the same friends. I'm lucky that I've got Alex and Emma as my best friends along with my friends from university.

Even though I haven't changed, other things have. I am a lottery winner and with boyfriends I have to be more cautious.

I used to think getting married would be a simple thing. Now, I have to consider that someone might want my money more than me. I could lose it, and that is a bit scary. I do want to get married one day, so thinking about the money does come into it. I have to secure my future and my children's future. I don't want someone to say, 'Thanks, this has been a lovely five -year marriage, see you later,' and walk away with my money.

When I say 'no' to men who ask me out, they say, 'It's because you are a lottery winner and you think you're better than me.' That's just not the case. If I turn them down, it is because I'm not attracted to them. Simple. But those excuses are easy for them to make.

I am an open and trusting person and I don't want to lose that. I don't find it easy to think the worst of people. So I am careful, but I don't let the concern bother me too much.

One day I will get married, and it will be to someone who loves me deeply. I will still have to ask that question about the money, but I'm pretty sure that I will know 'the one'. I always listen to my family's judgement, and my sisters are like a radar system for any guy I meet.

My sisters have been such a support to me, and would be if I was worth 1p. Paying for their boob operations was the first big thing I did after winning. Some winners buy flash cars and houses first. I bought two pairs of breasts!

The operations were going to cost £4,800 each, and my sisters were going to take out loans to pay for them.

Emma was really slim and had no cleavage after breast-feeding her son. Alex didn't have the breasts to match her size 12 curves. Emma went from a 30A to a 30C while Alex went from a 34B to a 34DD. I wasn't tempted myself because I've always been happy with the size of my breasts.

They were as excited about getting them done as I was about paying for them. I couldn't have them going into debt for this!

Three months after I won, they got their new boobs and haven't stopped smiling since.

It was one of the best things about winning the lottery. I bought my sisters some happiness and that felt brilliant. I know they would have done exactly the same for me, whatever I wanted.

My sisters are so important. Emma did my make-up, told me what to wear to school discos and looked out for me. She seemed so old. Alex and I used to play dolls together. As the middle girl, I got the best out of both of them. We have always been close and never fought. If you put us in a submarine and sank it, we would get along just fine.

It was brilliant to be able to buy my parents a detached home. I also bought myself a five-bedroom house for around £500,000, but I took a mortgage on that. I'm really conscious that this money is a godsend. I want to make it last. I don't live a flash lifestyle. Instead, I budget to live off a portion of the interest.

Moving out of my parents' home was difficult. I got my new house, put all my design touches in there, and it was perfect. Yet I couldn't bring myself to move in. It was only five minutes from my parents' place, but I kept making excuses about things not being ready. After about six months, I finally took the plunge. I now live in my own five-bedroom home. It sounds a bit weird when I say it. Such a grown-up thing, but I'm very proud of it.

I would like to go back to university and go on to get a job. It has been a fantastic time, but I'm coming up to the fifth anniversary of the win and have reached the point where I need more stimulation. I want to have a sense of purpose when I wake up in the morning. Now, I get up and think 'what shall I do today?' and I can do whatever I want.

There are only so many clothes you can buy. The shops don't change that much if you go every few days! I know I'm so lucky to be able to afford things, but I think I have more to give. I will enjoy going to work, being involved in something. As a lottery winner I may get criticised if I get a job, but I can't shop for ever.

I'm also a really social person. I can get a bit tired of doing things on my own. It's not that I get bored. I just enjoy being with other people.

I was interested in being a counsellor before I started the social work course, so I would like to do some training for that. By taking time out from university, I realised that the social work course wasn't right for me. Winning the lottery has given me other options.

I don't regret dropping out of university and taking the opportunities from the win. But I do want to be more involved in normal things. I'm a normal girl from a normal background. Having a job and settling down are natural things to me.

The money has given me and my family great security. It's been nice to help out those nearest and dearest. It was a huge amount of money to deal with, but I've had expert advice along the way and I'm a naturally cautious person. Most of it is safely invested, so I don't have to worry too much about it.

I've obviously treated myself along the way. Who wouldn't? Going into a shop and being able to afford almost everything in there is a good feeling. I must admit I bought a lot of clothes without trying them on. They are now in cupboards, still brand new. I'm going to give those away.

I also bought a Range Rover Sport without thinking too much. I don't like driving and can't park, so it was not the best move I've ever made. It was a waste of money. At least I can recognise that, and now know that I'm better off keeping things simple.

I'm back to a Mini convertible now and very happy with that. The money has been fantastic. I've had some great times, great memories, and now my family and I are secure. But I value my friends and family above any bank balance and that will never change. I'm still an ordinary girl from Whitley Bay.

It has been a bit of whirlwind but it is slowing down now. Before long I'll be settled down in a job and probably married. But if there's a chance for a photo shoot and having my hair and make-up done, I'll be there.

Top Ten Luckiest Jobs

Anyone can win the lottery but people in certain types of job have won more often that others. Here are the top ten jobs:

Construction workers (builders)
Administration staff
Management
Drivers (lorries, buses and taxis)
Catering (chefs and pub workers)
Factory workers
Customer service and retail
Financial sector (accountancy and banks)
Care, charity and social work
IT, computing and electronics

The Lucky Hairdressers

Seven hairdressers from the Smile salon in Glasgow won £2,928,483 on a Lucky Dip ticket in a Wednesday draw in February 2007. Syndicate leader Wendy Brown, 39, and her colleagues each received £418,354.71.

We'd always dreamed about what we'd do when we won the lottery. We talked about it quite a lot. Everyone loved a bit of gossip about the game, the winners and how to spend the money. It took our minds off things when there were bills to pay and it was pouring with rain outside.

We worked in a busy salon on the outskirts of Glasgow city centre What with the hairdryers going and people chatting away, it was always a lively place. It wasn't a fancy, designer salon with huge price tags. It was just a good, normal hairdresser's. We had customers of all ages, and they were all friends.

We all had to work because we needed the money, but we were lucky that we had a lot of fun and got on well together. It was a great place to work. There was always something to say and always a laugh to be had.

Mary the cleaner, who was 77 at the time, and I loved to imagine what we'd do when we won the lottery. We joked we'd meet up at Glasgow Airport and get the first plane out to somewhere sunny. In our minds we would be jetting off to the Caribbean or Florida. Then we'd buy big cars, big houses, clothes and champagne. The customers would join in and we'd all have a laugh as our imaginations ran wild.

The syndicate of the group of us who pooled our money together had been going for ages, almost since the lottery started more than 15 years ago. It was made up of Lorna, Natalie and Megan, all hairdressers, Mary the cleaner, two other colleagues and me. I did the beauty treatments and nails in the salon.

Lorna and I had been around for about eleven years, Natalie had been at the salon about eight years and Megan was the 'new girl'. There were seven of us in the syndicate – a crucial number that I will return to later – and we each put in £2 a week for 14 Lucky Dip tickets. Ten on Saturday and four on Wednesday.

We were making around £250 a week, depending on how many hours we did. Not bad, but we weren't living like pop stars.

I was living with my boyfriend (living in sin as Lorna would say). Lorna was married with a little girl, and Natalie was two weeks away from getting married. Megan was pregnant and had just bought a house. *K 195,492*

As the salon was always so busy, with back-to-back bookings, we rarely got breaks. The great thing was that the people who came in were really nice. We'd done the hair of many of them for ages and some even came in twice a week. We got to know them well and heard all about their families. We had a good reputation, and that counts for everything in hairdressing.

Even so, we all had moments when we would pause and look out the windows. We'd watch the world go by and dream of better places where the Glasgow rain couldn't reach.

We'd won a few tenners from the lottery over the years, and that was really exciting. Then one Friday there was a rumour spreading fast of a big win in Glasgow. What's more, it had gone to a hairdressing salon.

Everyone in hairdressing phoned each

other, trying to find out who'd won. The girls wondered who the lucky winners were and if we knew them.

They never imagined it was us, and that was my fault. I had the winning ticket in my pocket. I didn't realise right away and then, when I did, I was in such a state of shock that I couldn't tell the others. I can't explain what happened to me. I just froze.

I normally check the tickets the day after the draw, but this Wednesday I put them in my jacket pocket and forgot they were there.

On Friday, I happened to wear the same jacket and discovered them scrunched up in a pocket as I was going across the road to the shops to get some milk and lunch for the girls. I got the girl in the shop to check the tickets..

'Go on,' I joked. 'Make me a millionaire.' I've never said that before and had no idea why I was saying it then. The first two tickets came back with nothing.

I said, 'Third time lucky.'

The girl put the ticket in and her face suddenly changed. She looked at me and said, 'I've never seen that before. The machine's saying you've got to phone Camelot.' She gave me the ticket and I just walked away.

The girl later told me the fact that I'd won

just didn't register for me. I just said 'OK' and walked out. She said to the lady behind me, 'I think she's just won the lottery.' I was in a daze and didn't hear a word.

I came back to work and acted normal, although I was very quiet. I just walked back in and hung my jacket up. The girls said, 'Did you not get any lunch?'

I replied, 'I'm not hungry.' I must have been in shock.

They thought it was weird, but we were busy and we just got on with looking after the customers. It was really odd because, as the news of a Glasgow win started to go round and people rang up to check, the girls were still talking about what they would do if they were the lucky ones. What to do with £200,000 or so and how lucky those winners were. Natalie was talking about getting a BMW X5, worth £50,000. Lorna was saying she would go to Florida. If only it was us!

The phones continued to buzz as everyone desperately tried to find out who'd won. The girls phoned friends and told them they hadn't won.

All this time I was walking around like a zombie with the winning ticket in my jacket pocket. I went downstairs to where I did the beauty treatments. I did someone's nails but for once barely spoke to the customer.

I can't describe how it felt other than being detached from everything around. I knew I had promised to tell 77-year-old Mary first if we won, but she wasn't in the salon then. That was the only thought I could focus on.

I finished the client's nails and then went straight upstairs to telephone Mary.

I don't know why I didn't tell everyone at the same time. There was just this urge in my head: phone Mary, phone Mary. Beyond that, I couldn't think.

I got through to her and just said, 'Mary, we've won the lottery.'

'Don't say that to me, hen,' she replied.

The phone is by the main salon so everyone heard. It stopped the salon dead, customers and staff. The hairdryers stopped, everyone looked at me and I remember dropping the phone. Everyone started screaming as they realised we had won.

Everybody was so excited. We were yelling and hugging each other and the customers were cheering. Everyone was wondering how much we'd won but we couldn't work out if we'd got £29,000, £200,000 or what. There were too many noughts! I phoned my

24

boyfriend Paul to check. He found out that we'd won £418,000 each. It was an amazing feeling. We couldn't stop smiling, shouting and screaming.

One moment the salon had been a gentle buzz of activity and the next, chaos. We'd won. We really had won!

News got out straight away. It is not every day you see a group of girls going mad in a hairdressing salon, is it?

So many people were happy for us, and it felt so good. Strangers walked past giving thumbs up and drivers beeped their horns. Locals said how great it was to know a winner, and how happy they were that one of their 'own' had won. They were thrilled for us because they knew us and felt part of a family.

I had to go outside to phone Camelot because it was so noisy in the salon. The others watched me through the window and said I was chatting away holding the ticket on top of a rubbish bin. It was quite windy, so there was a bit of a panic that the winning ticket would blow away.

It took a while to get through. Finally, a girl answered and said her name was Bonnie. I shouted, 'Bonnie Scotland!' I think I might have been a bit delirious.

None of us could stop smiling. When I went over to the supermarket to get some champagne, everyone was asking if it was true we'd won the lottery. It was clear without me saying a word!

We carried on working, though some of the clients were a bit worried that we might slice their ears off because we were so excited. They just had a blow-dry instead of letting our shaking hands do haircuts or nail treatments.

We had the radio on and they were talking about the win on there too. It is incredible to hear people talking about lottery winners on the news and to realise that it is actually you they are talking about. They even played a record for us.

We celebrated, of course, but we had two wedding parties coming in for styling the next day and couldn't let them down. They phoned to see if we would still be working and were a bit worried, but it was never a question. We opened up as usual though it is a bit of a different feeling when you turn up on a Saturday morning as a lottery winner.

I remember catching the bus into work that day as usual and thinking, 'My God, it really is me.'

I don't think I ate for about three days. I

must have done, but it was all a bit of a daze. Lorna cried a lot out of happiness, and all of us noticed our huge smiles when we caught our reflections in the salon mirrors.

It was a funny, weird and wonderful experience.

But it took a while to sink in. I remember walking around the shops in a trance looking for a new outfit to buy for the Camelot cheque presentation. There was stuff I could easily afford, but I was still checking the price tag and putting things back. Megan bought two tops and spent about £50. That seemed really extravagant. Normally we would be saving up for a couple of months to buy one top as a treat.

We got the money on Monday, and posed for the press with our big cheque on Tuesday. It felt strange having photographers taking pictures of us and seeing ourselves in the local papers, but it was fun.

We really were lottery winners, but we all still had a nagging doubt that it wasn't real. We kept thinking that we were locked in a very vivid dream and would wake up with the alarm call to go into work.

Camelot gave us champagne in some very nice glasses with the lottery logo on the side of them. Megan asked if we could buy them and someone said, 'No, you are winners, they are yours to keep.' That's when we knew we really had won.

All those plans about flying away never happened because, after the cheque presentation, we carried on working as normal. I know I said I'd be on the first plane out of Glasgow, but we all felt a duty to our customers and the salon. We didn't want to let people down. They had been loyal to us and we weren't going to quit overnight. We were still just normal girls, and we weren't going to drop everything.

Lorna said we should all go away for a weekend to celebrate together, and we regret not doing that now.

The win hasn't changed us as people – we still talk and gossip endlessly – but it sure did make a difference to our lives.

Megan and Lorna called each other from garage showrooms when they were looking for cars. They couldn't believe what they were doing and that they could afford them.

Lorna bought a Honda Civic and got her husband an even bigger car. I can't drive yet, but I bought my dad a car. Natalie got her X5 and Megan got an Audi. Natalie and Megan paid off the mortgages on their houses and Lorna did her house up beautifully. She had a five-year plan to do one room at a time, but she did it all in five months.

I don't think our lives have fully changed. If we had each won millions, it might have been different, but what we won was just enough. We never got any hassle, and no bother from people wanting money off us.

The win gave us great security, but we couldn't afford to give up work completely. That money would soon go if we didn't look after it. Megan was just 21, so it wouldn't stretch over her lifetime. We did some great things with holidays, cars and houses, but then we had to get on with life. We didn't want to give up on work anyhow. Shopping all day every day actually gets boring!

The salon was doing well, but it was owned by one of the syndicate members who wanted to retire, so she decided to sell it. We lost our jobs there, but Natalie was keen to open a new salon and found a good site only about 10 minutes from the old salon After a complete makeover, it was ready to open. It was an easy decision for all of us to keep working with her and to stay together.

The great thing was that loads of our

customers followed us. We wondered how we would do, and worried that people would think we didn't need the business because we were lottery winners. Luckily, they were loyal. We were glad, because we would have missed them. They were part of our lives and it would have been strange to walk away from that.

Sticking together and having each other has made it easier for us. I think it might be hard if you are a big winner on your own. We can talk to each other about what we are doing and what is happening. It is fantastic when you have a group of girls who just understand each other. That is so precious that we never want to abandon it.

People say it is pure luck that you win, but I think there might be more to it. As I said before, the number 7 featured largely in our win.

I went to a fortune teller in Glasgow. He told me the number 7 would be important in a lottery win. When I put my own tickets on, I did 7, 14, 28 and so on but never won a penny.

I totally forgot about the fortune teller until we won, and the number 7 connections kept stacking up.

The win was seven years almost to the day

that I went to see the fortune teller. He had given me a book and signed it with the date, so I knew exactly.

There were seven of us in the syndicate. Mary was 77, I was 37, and some of the girls had birthdays and anniversaries on the 7th. We won in 2007. There were even sevens in our car registration numbers. I'd bought some feng shui candles ages ago and decided to light them at the New Year for good luck. I'd bought them on a visit to the United States and, when I looked at my passport, it was seven years since that trip. I'd had them for seven years! The number 7 just cropped up everywhere.

Added to that, I broke a mirror at work. I phoned my boyfriend to say we were going to get seven years of bad luck, but he said it signalled new beginnings, fresh luck. That was on Tuesday, the day before we won the lottery. It makes you wonder.

Superstition or not, the win has been fantastic for us. We have great family security. Lorna has had another baby girl, and Natalie is now the boss and has a daughter. We've all been able to help our families and pay off mortgages, so we are secure. We couldn't be happier.

We've been able to do some great things,

the sort of things you only ever dream about.

I took my parents and nephew on a fantastic 14-night cruise. The girls have been to the Caribbean, Florida, Las Vegas, Dubai and Menorca.

Natalie went to Mauritius for her honeymoon just weeks after the win although it was already planned. She didn't change anything. Customers asked why she didn't fly first class. She said it would have cost another £8,000 for a first-class seat and that was an awful lot of money to pay for a chair! Lorna went with her daughter to Lapland and saw the real Father Christmas, so she was very happy.

The best thing is having security but still coming into work. We appreciate everything we have gained from the win, but the customers and our families keep us grounded.

It would be boring without the others and without work. We are lucky that we get on so well and have such a good time. Natalie is a good boss and really laid back.

None of us could imagine not seeing each other. Moving away into big houses and getting on with our lives separately could never happen.

You might be tempted to stop work if you won £1 million, but I have a sneaky feeling we'd all still be here working if we won £10 million. Maybe not full time though!

We read about one lottery winner who had won millions and had been on so many holidays he couldn't remember them. Can you imagine that? We don't want to go on holiday all the time.

The maddest thing we did was give a taxi driver an £80 tip on the way home from picking up the cheque.

But life goes on. We all have the usual ups and downs of family life and relationships. That is just real life. We have been very lucky and the lottery has been brilliant for us, but we also think we are lucky to have our friendship, families and health.

We still pinch ourselves about it all. If we ever get talking about the win, the excitement and joy flood back. We'd all like to go back to that day and experience it again. It would be great to have had CCTV in the shop to capture our reactions because it was so fantastic.

It would make brilliant viewing. We relive that scene in our minds all the time.

Top Ten Places to Hide the Winning Ticket

Hanging on to the ticket once your numbers have come up is one of the worst problems for winners. It is a balance between keeping it safe and remembering where you have put it. Here are some places lottery winners have used to keep their prize-winning ticket secure.

Inside a bra
Under the mattress
Under a fax machine at work
Stapled to a shirt pocket
In the dog's basket
In the microwave
Under a flowerpot
In a biscuit jar
In a sock or shoe
Under a chessboard

The Oldest Winner

Retired car plant worker Bob Bradley, a World War II veteran, won £3,570,063, on his 83rd birthday in March 2006 but died a year later. He gave £1 million each to his son Barry, 61, and his grandson Chris, 38, who tells his story.

Bob's legacy is what I see around me. We're living in a five-bedroom house in a stunning village in the Welsh countryside thanks to him. We've got four acres of beautiful gardens. This place is fantastic.

We used to live in a three-bedroom terrace. Nice, but nothing like this. We've got so much space now. I'm just converting the garage into a snooker room with a spiral staircase that connects it to the house.

The lottery has been brilliant for us.

We used to dream of living in this area. There just weren't enough years in our lives to be able to earn and save enough money to buy up here.

My dad lives in another great house and neither of us has to work. In the past, we worked hard and struggled with money. It is great to have that feeling of pressure lifted now, and it's all thanks to my granddad.

Bob was a simple but wonderful guy. The sort of bloke everyone loves bumping into. He would have a chat with you, would always have time for you and would always offer to help you out.

You needed some painting done? Bob was your man. Needed help with the gardening? Bob would be there before you had finished the sentence. As long as he got a sandwich and a cup of tea, he'd be fine.

He loved helping people. I expect everyone knows someone like Bob.

He was my grandfather so I'm biased, but he was one of the good guys.

It was such a shock when he won – to him and to us. He was just an ordinary bloke who had worked all his life without moaning. For some reason you don't expect people like that to get lucky and win the lottery.

He started out his career earning 20p a week. In his whole life he never earned more than £150 a week. Now he was a millionaire.

His first thought was to make sure the win

helped his family. That was his true delight of being a lottery winner: seeing his family happy. He told us, 'I want nothing for myself but everything for my family.'

My dad, Barry, worked on relining water mains. He was away from home during the week for more than 20 years. It was a tough and tiring job, so to be able to walk away from it was such a relief for him. I'm not sure how much longer he could have kept going.

He would be up at 4 a.m. on Monday to get to where he was working by 8 a.m. Then he would work solid and live in lodgings until Friday afternoon when he could come home to my mum, Yvonne. Week in, week out. Year in, year out.

I was really interested in cars and went to college to do mechanics. I didn't finish the course because I got married at 18. At 16, I fell in love when I saw Geraldine in the hairdresser's where she worked. She jokes that I used to come in twice a week to get my hair cut!

After leaving college, I followed my dad into a job on the water mains. I too would be away from Monday to Friday. Because the job paid decent money (more than I could get anywhere else at the time), we had to sacrifice a bit of family life to build for the future.

Geraldine and I got a flat together when our son Lee was born. We saved hard and then bought a nice little terraced house in Llanelli for £35,000. We did it up ourselves, and Bob was always there to lend a helping hand. He was my granddad, but he was more like a mate helping out.

We soon had a second child, Zara. Being away was taking its toll on the family, so I got a job closer to home. Geraldine had started running a hair salon and worked very long hours.

My being at home made family life easier, but we were still working all hours. It was a constant juggling act between making the money and bringing up the kids.

Both my dad and I were struggling and needed a break.

Bob wanted to make sure our dreams came true. He didn't want us to have to worry about money, and he got so much pleasure from helping us out. So it was so incredibly sad when he passed away just a year after his win.

There is a huge void where he was. I'm not sure I can do him justice. He was just so important in our lives. From when I was a little boy, all the way to when I became a man, he was always there for me.

Material things didn't matter to Bob. He would go around in his painting clothes and not worry about what he looked like. He would take me for walks picking blackberries and enjoying the countryside for free. It was brilliant for me as a lad because he had so many stories and was always fun.

He liked being busy and helping others because he loved being with people. He used to go to the social club with my grandma Mim, and they went on holidays with friends as a break from work. He worked as a machine operator in a car accessories plant and my grandma worked at a radiator factory, both in Llanelli.

Like so many from his generation, he was a modest guy and didn't like any fuss. He served in World War II with the Royal Welch Regiment and was involved in the D-Day landings, but never really talked about it.

You had to quiz him and quiz him for the smallest bit of information about the war. I thought it was a subject I probably shouldn't bring up. We did manage to find out that one of his friends was blown up in front of him in Italy, and that he had shrapnel wounds.

He had letters and medals that I took into school. They didn't mean much to him though. What did he need them for when he'd lost a good friend?

But it was his duty to fight in the war and he never complained about that.

He was a real character. When I was younger I got a bike for Christmas. I remember him tying it to the back of his motorbike with a length of rope and giving me a ride along the road.

When I had kids, he did similar things. He put them on the back of his motorbike, tied them on with strong rope and drove off. They had crash helmets on and he was a safe driver. He made sure they wouldn't fall off by tying their hands and legs to the motorbike. You couldn't get away with that now!

But that's the way he had always done it. It was safe in his mind. He took me down to the docks tied onto the back of his pushbike, so it was natural he would do the same with his great-grandkids.

He retired from the factories after more than 40 years of loyal service. But he could not sit still. Taking it easy was not for him. He enjoyed his rugby, going to the club and going to restaurants every now and again. He was still around in a flash if there were any jobs that needed doing.

When my grandma Mim died, we started to build an extension so that Bob could move in with us. He didn't want to be on his own. Geraldine's salon was doing well, so we had managed to move into another terrace house. We had more room and were happy to offer it to him.

The funny thing about all this is that Mim always did the lottery, played bingo and did the scratchcards. She wanted to win for the family but she didn't have much luck. It was Bob, who wasn't really that bothered, who won the jackpot two years after she died.

He used to pick his numbers carefully, mind you. If a number came up on Wednesday, he wouldn't use it on Saturday, and so on. They were always random numbers though.

It was his 83rd birthday when he hit the jackpot. He was so active and young in his outlook that he didn't like to be reminded about birthdays. He didn't like people knowing how old he was, so he didn't want to go out that night. He would not budge, so we left him to it.

He watched the draw on TV and thought he had four numbers. He phoned my mum and dad but we were all out. He just left messages saying he thought he'd won the lottery.

He didn't phone us in the morning because we were supposed to be going motocross racing. Our son Lee competed in races most weekends. Bob didn't know how much he'd won then, but he didn't want to bother us.

Mind you, I think he would have been the same even if he had known. He would have thought, '£3 million, oh that can wait till they're back.'

That kind of money didn't make sense to a working-class man who had been in the war. When he only made £150 a week at the peak of his career, you can imagine how difficult it was to explain £3.5 million to him.

He did not understand what that money could do and what he could afford. We wrote it down and showed him all the noughts. It still didn't make any sense to him. He liked his motorbikes so we said he could now afford at least five Ferraris. That still didn't click.

He said, 'Well, OK, what do I give you?'

I said, 'It's up to you, Gramps. If you want to give £50, give £50.'

'Would you be happy with £50?' he asked.

I said, 'Yes, I didn't have it yesterday, so I'd be happy with that.'

He had a bit of think and said £1 million for my dad and £1 million for me. 'That sounds about right,' he said. It was incredibly generous of him. To this day I don't think he realised how much it was. The one thing that really mattered to him was seeing his family doing OK.

He got advice about investing the money but the first thing he bought was a pet rabbit for Zara. That cost £8.50.

Then he bought this country house for us, and a house and Mercedes for my dad. He also splashed out on a luxury motorhome so we could support Lee as a family at motocross races across the country.

Bob never really changed his ways. I suppose you don't if money has been tight all your life. After his win, we went into a shoe shop and found a great pair of shoes for him, all leather. He tried them on and they fitted like a glove, he said.

When he found out they were £80, he started saying they were rubbing a bit and pinching. He said we should buy a pair for Zara instead. He really didn't want to spend the money on himself. We made him get them though, and he did love those shoes.

When he came to live with us, he was such

good company. He could never sit still for long though. Even in his eighties, he mowed the lawn and did some building work.

One day, I was replacing some slates on the roof and he was helping me out. I had to get some supplies, so I told him to do nothing until I came back.

Of course, he tried to do it on his own and fell through the roof. He made Lee swear not to tell me. When I come back he was sitting with his foot up.

'What's the matter with you?' I asked.

He said, 'Oh, nothing, just having a rest.'

Lee eventually told me. We tried to get him to go to hospital but he wouldn't. He didn't want to wait around, and he said there were other people that needed treatment more than him. Absolutely typical.

There were no strings attached to the money he gave. He didn't ask for anything. He just wanted to be part of his family, and he already was whether he had three pounds or £3 million.

He was always having a laugh with the kids. He hired a helicopter to take Lee and his mates to their school prom. It even made the newspapers. I've never been up in one of them, he said, so Bob went along for the ride.

We took him to the Royal Welsh Show, which he'd never been to. He was really taken with the Jacuzzi. The guy said he could try it out if he liked. Bob being Bob, he jumped in wearing his pants!

Bob was an incredible man. It is still difficult to come to terms with him not being here.

He had just been to Turkey on holiday. He came back and said he had felt a bit tired at the airport. We suggested he stay home while we went to a race meeting the next morning. But he insisted on coming along. We now think he knew something was up and wanted to be with his family if he was passing on.

It happened about 2 a.m. He woke up feeling a bit breathless and got Lee to rub his back. As usual he told Lee not to wake us up, but Lee did.

Bob stepped outside for some fresh air, but then he startled to struggle with his breathing. He was changing colour. It was 45 minutes before the ambulance came. We were desperate and worked on keeping him alive the whole time. He squeezed our hands. He was letting us know how much he loved us. We just felt helpless.

He was still breathing when he went in the

ambulance, but he died shortly afterwards at the hospital.

It was devastating beyond belief. We were glad that he didn't suffer much, but it was so terrible to lose someone who had been so close and important all our lives. He was a joker. You were always laughing or crying with laughter with Bob, and all of a sudden he wasn't around.

It has taken us a long time to deal with his death. To be honest, we'll never completely get over it.

The great sorrow is that Bob didn't have time to enjoy his win for longer. At least in the year he did have, he fully enjoyed himself. He did things he never could have done before and saw places he never would have seen.

There was nothing wasted in his life. He would have had no regrets apart from wanting to be with us for longer. We have the same regret. There is a massive gap now, like losing your best mate. We were always together, round the fairs, marts and antiques shops.

Bob was a little bit like a ragamuffin and, fittingly, he died in his working clothes. It was a tough moment when I was cleaning out the garage the other day and found his painting clothes.

We were still grieving six days after his death when a massive tax demand from the Inland Revenue landed on the doormat. Completely out of the blue.

It was a huge amount and there was no appeal, no leeway. We had to pay up in six months or else.

It was awful coming so close after his death. The amount didn't bother us as much as the speed of the demand did. It was really horrible.

Bob's winnings, as well as everything he owned, were subject to inheritance tax. What's more, everything he gave away, out of the goodness of his heart, also had to be taxed. The rules are very strict. The tax amount goes down steadily over seven years but, because Bob died in the first year, the top amount had to be paid.

Luckily, Bob went to his grave knowing only that he'd looked after us. We don't let the tax sour our memories either. We are still in a fantastic financial position thanks to Bob.

As well as the money he gave us, he left us with some brilliant memories.

Camelot organises events so you get the chance to meet other winners. We went to the celebrations at Somerset House in London for the 2,000th millionaire created by the lottery.

Bob was on top form. When a group of us

winners from Wales had our pictures taken for the press, he clambered on to a table and sang, 'I'm on top of the world.'

The Camelot people got a bit worried and said, 'Get him down from there. He's our oldest winner and we don't want him to get hurt.'

He just laughed. He was some character.

It has been great to meet other winners through Camelot and share our stories and experiences. We are all on the same level, all from working-class families. Our lives have changed so much. The win has given us an easier life, security and a great start for the kids. That's a common thing about winners. It's not about the flash cars and big mansions. It is about the basics of taking care of the family.

That's the sort of sentiment Bob would approve of. He gave generously and set his family up for life. Wherever he is and whatever he's doing, Bob will be happy with that.

Unusual Purchases by Lottery Winners

Most lottery winners buy houses and cars and indulge themselves, family and friends with luxury holidays. But having new spending power has resulted in some unusual purchases by winners such as:

A gastric band for the wife
A pair of new knees
A hair salon
A racehorse
A Robin Reliant
Woodland and 300 new trees
Breast enlargements for sisters
A flock of sheep
A whiskey factory
A 'lady' title

The Belfast Bus Driver

Bus driver and community worker Peter Lavery, 48, was one of the first 'big' winners when he scooped £10,248,233 in May 1995, just six months after the National Lottery was launched.

If you heard my life story from the start, you wouldn't say I was lucky. I was brought up in a loving but working-class family in East Belfast. The Troubles was a way of life. Troops with guns on street corners were as much a part of the landscape as lamp posts.

I worked on the buses in Belfast, driving on the roads that became infamous on news bulletins for all the wrong reasons. I was hijacked, robbed seven times and had a close friend who suffered 70 per cent burns after his bus was fire-bombed. A week earlier I had been driving that route, so it could easily have been me.

But then, completely out of the blue, I won the lottery. It was week 79. I'd put £2 on each week since it started, so I'd paid out £158. I got back … £10.2 million!

It was a staggering sum of money. I went from being a bus driver to a multi-millionaire in a flash. One day I was working and the next I was on a beach in the Caribbean. That beach trip cost £60,000. That was more than four years' wages. On one holiday.

There was never anything flash about me. I lived in a terrace house, but now I could afford a luxury mansion. I never had enough to buy my own car, but suddenly I could get two cars for £44,000. That's almost three years' wages.

The size of the lottery win shocked me. I kept repeating, 'Is this a dream?'

The change in circumstances is hard to grasp, especially when you never had much except bills to pay.

I shook my head at times and was sometimes scared to go to sleep. I didn't want to wake up and have to clock in for work again.

But it was real all right. Peter Lavery the bus driver had become Peter Lavery the multi-millionaire. There was no going back.

I didn't have a dull life before the win. I was happy with family and friends, and loved working for my community. I even met US President Bill Clinton when I visited the White

House in Washington, DC, with other Belfast community leaders.

But, whatever your background, £10.2 million is a massive amount. You need to know a bit more about my life to realise just how much it meant to me and my family.

I'm from a family of three brothers and two sisters. We were brought up in the Short Strand area of Belfast. Our dad, Charles, was a fitter but didn't work for a while due to ill health. There's no point denying that things were tight.

We were a happy family despite not having much money. We had loads of love and affection instead. Home was a noisy, lively and fun place to be.

Our mum Rita would always see that we were looked after. Then, if she had a penny left, she would put it in the poor box. She believed there was always someone worse off. She would give away the last penny in her purse to help people less fortunate. That has always stuck with me.

Mum died when I was 16. We were all devastated and it was difficult to deal with. Dad took over and really looked after the family from that moment on. He died just 14 months before I won.

It has been terrible not having my parents around to share the joy of the win. They worked so hard and made so many sacrifices to make sure we all had a good life. They deserved to be part of this, but I guess it was just not to be. It still makes me sad. They both went too early.

That's why I set up the Rita and Charles Trust in memory of my parents to raise funds for deserving causes.

I love the people of Belfast. They are very special to have come through so much and still have a great spirit about them. I'm honoured to be able to help them and put some of the lottery money to good use.

I've helped raise more than £1 million for charity since the win. The best part is the annual Christmas party we put on for around 400 working-class elderly people. These are people who may not get that much company during the festive period. It is heart breaking to see some of them alone over Christmas with no family and no money. It is great to bring them some happiness. I'm so proud of that.

It is very humbling when these people, who have been through so much, say to me, 'You've made my Christmas.'

The city is part of me and I couldn't just

spend my money and leave. That would be a betrayal of everything my parents stood for and how they brought me up. It would also be a massive snub to Belfast. I could never do that. I've spent most of my life saying how good the Belfast people are, so to leave them would be wrong.

People who know about the times of trouble on the streets probably expect me to be living in Florida or on a Caribbean island. But they never grew up here, so they don't know the hold this place has on people.

I was born in 1961 and The Troubles began seriously in 1969, so I grew up with them.

Every day we'd see soldiers on the street and big armoured vans driving around. We didn't look twice because this was normal. If we saw a road blocked off, we just walked on because that type of thing happened every day. You don't wait and watch.

We just adapted to it. What could we do? You couldn't lock yourself in the house.

Of course, everyone knows someone who suffered: a family member, a friend or a friend of a friend. When I was ten years old my friend's mother was blown up in a pub. But, thankfully, none of my direct family experienced anything really bad. We just focused on surviving.

I wouldn't change my childhood. It is part of who I am and made me strong. I never give up now. In a sense I'm stubborn once I get going on something. That's OK, because you have to be like that if you want to succeed in business or make a difference in the community.

When I was younger, I didn't get on at school. Everyone else in the family has a good education, but it just didn't work for me. I was short-sighted and couldn't see the board. I didn't want to admit that, so I sat at the back. It was clear that I was not going to learn properly.

The day I left school was one of the happiest days of my life. I walked out on a Friday and started an apprenticeship as a plumber on Monday. Brilliant.

Growing up in Belfast was different to other cities in the UK. As a teenager, you were more or less confined to the area where you lived. You didn't really go into town, or to another area, because you were likely to get beaten up. We had community centres and youth clubs in the area, and people stayed where they felt safe. It seems strange now with the Belfast city centre such a bright and lively place.

I was still a happy boy with lots of friends. We all got involved at the local community centre. I started to go as a youngster. Then I helped put on entertainment and work with the community. I felt such a part of the area that it seemed natural to help.

I had no idea then that I would go on to become chairman for ten years, and the first Catholic chairman, of the East Belfast Community Centre Council, an umbrella organisation for more than 200 community and voluntary groups.

There were a lot of people who helped. We all got mentioned in our parliament for contributing towards community understanding.

The community work was my passion. I loved meeting people and talking to them. It was the same on the buses. You'd meet nice people on both sides of the divide.

I have great memories of those days. My friends from the buses are still friends now.

Bus hijackings were sadly common at times. If someone wanted the bus, you gave them the bus. They never got big money. The most would be about £20, no fortunes.

There was one driver who had a bomb thrown through his windscreen. It ended up in his lap and he got 70 per cent burns. He was badly scarred.

But you didn't dwell on the bad stuff. If you did, you wouldn't go to work, and then you couldn't pay your bills. You had to be positive and thankful it wasn't you.

Everyone had their bad times and scares. I'd prefer to remember the good days and the good people. The spirit is incredible and the laughter is never far away with the people of Belfast.

One of our guys got hijacked and was told to drive to City Hall. The hijackers said there was a bomb on board. Our guy drove down to the bus depot canteen instead. When his mates asked why later, he said, 'You lot are always complaining about the canteen so I thought I'd help you out.' Thankfully, there was no bomb.

Laughter and tears, that's Belfast.

The biggest day of my life came in 1995 when I met President Bill Clinton at a conference in Washington. He was keen to help Northern Ireland. He wanted to understand all he could to help bring about peace. There were hundreds of guests and there was a big marquee on the White House lawn with food and entertainment. It was amazing to be there. Me, a little old bus driver from Belfast, and the

President of the United States. We all got to shake his hand and he spoke about helping. He seemed very genuine.

I thought that was as good as it got. But exactly a year later, to the day, it got even better.

I won the lottery.

It was just another week on the Belfast buses. I got a call from my sister to tell me I'd won, but I thought it was a joke. I didn't even believe her when she called again.

I got up in a daze the next morning. My sister, brother and I put the TV on and looked at the numbers. There was one lucky winner, and it was me! I couldn't believe it. The ticket shook in my hand.

I couldn't find the phone number for Camelot so had to spend 15p on Directory Inquiries. When I got through, they checked the details, but they couldn't confirm the win until someone had seen the ticket in person.

I had to go to work because I had two routes to do that day. I drove around with the ticket in my pocket. It was incredible to think I had a piece of paper worth £10 million in my pocket. I was a bit scared something would happen to it.

Halfway through the second route, it

started sinking in. Here I was, 35 years old, and I didn't have to work again. What a feeling. My legs started going numb and I couldn't concentrate. I hit a ramp and bumped over it. One of the passengers said, 'Didn't you see that ramp?'

'To tell you the truth, no I didn't,' I replied. I was in shock.

I got back and asked for the next Monday off. I just put 'personal reasons' on the form but I knew I would never go back.

I remember the moment Camelot put the ticket through the machine and it confirmed that I was a multi-millionaire. My knees hit the floor and the tears came then. It is hard to believe that a piece of paper can be worth so much.

The day I won, 33 million people had bought tickets. 33 million! And I was the lucky one.

It's a scary and amazing feeling. I just remember thinking it would be the end to uncertainty. My family would be able to move and everyone would be all right.

At first, I worried that people around would be jealous. I thought they wouldn't talk to me or would say things behind my back. But everyone was really good. I think people were just pleased that someone from Northern Ireland had won.

I remember a guy called Karl Crompton won the jackpot three weeks before I did. It was all over the place because he was a young, good-looking lad. At the time, I thought, 'Some day that is going to be me.' I didn't expect it to be just three weeks later though.

With that sort of money in the bank, I chucked my job in and treated myself and all my family. My own lifestyle has changed beyond belief. I've swapped a three-bedroom terrace for a luxury, five-bedroom home on the outskirts of Belfast and another one on the coast.

There are not many bus drivers who can say they've been to Florida 20 times, New York, Boston and Las Vegas. I've also enjoyed 25 cruises and have flown on Concorde.

I've got two Jags, a Mercedes, a Lexus, an old Jeep and a DeLorean, the same as the car featured in the movie Back to the Future. It was made in Belfast and is one of the few still around.

For me the lottery has always been about making life better for me, my family and the people of Belfast.

As I got the cheque book out, I knew that I

had to use the money to help charity. I would enjoy my own share, but I wouldn't just let the money sit there and live off it.

Everything my mum and dad had brought me up to believe demanded that I did not waste this chance. I could not squander it all on myself. Don't get me wrong: I enjoy the luxuries in life, but I'm not a man of leisure.

I run a property firm and two local stores. I also have a company called Danny Boy, which has its own whiskey, crafts and gifts that are marketed and sold to raise money for charities.

I've got ambitions for all my businesses. I really want one of my stores to sell someone a jackpot-winning ticket one day. That would be amazing.

I've worked hard to build the property business up, so it is worth a lot. Even though the recent recession has wiped out some of its value, I'm still ahead.

I really don't like sitting still. That can be a bit of a curse, and is how I came to fall off the roof of my house five years ago.

I could have died. I went flying down the roof headfirst. If it hadn't been for my older brother, Joe, flipping me over I would have landed on my head and wouldn't be here now.

I'd gone up to clean the gutters and slipped.

I came down like on a kids' slide. I took off and thought I was going to meet my father and mother earlier than I expected. I thought the party was over and it was the end of this life, but my right foot took all the impact. You could hear the crunch as I landed. It just shattered.

I jumped up in shock with the adrenalin and Joe sat me down until the ambulance came. I lost a lot of blood and had to have transfusions. It was touch and go. My blood pressure dropped and I was semi-conscious in the ambulance.

They didn't know if they could save the leg. I woke up full of tubes and lines and couldn't feel anything from the waist down. I had to ask if I still had my leg.

The doctors, nurses and all the staff were amazing. I had four operations to rebuild the foot, including grafting muscle, flesh and a vein from my thigh. I was in hospital for six weeks and in a wheelchair for another 13.

You feel down and sorry for yourself, but soon realise that there are others worse off. It did shake me since I could have gone then. Now I'm even more determined than ever to look after my family, help charity and enjoy my life.

Sometimes it does feel a bit of a responsibility. The thought of £10 million gives me a shiver, but you can't really think too much about it. You do the lottery to win, so you have to be prepared to deal with it whether you win £10 or £10 million.

Winning the jackpot has given me the opportunity to do many things in my life. I've been able to look after the family, do charity work in our parents' name and see the world. I've got nice cars and nice houses and, if I want to take tomorrow off, I can. I don't have to ask anyone. Mind you, I'm three stones heavier than I was, but you can't be someone you're not. I've had 14 great years and they have gone by in a flash.

I've suffered in property through the recession but not as bad as some. My home was worth £2.5 million but, even though that price has dipped, it is still worth much more than the £750,000 I spent on buying it and doing it up.

I've never sat back, and I'm really proud that I've made that lottery jackpot work. I've done well as a businessman, making money from my shops. Danny Boy is proving successful at raising funds for charity. I've even launched my own whiskey called Danny Boy. It is not just a rich man's toy. Everything I set up is to make money and be successful.

I may be a jackpot winner but I approach life as a businessman. I worry when things don't work out. I worry about property values going down and I get the jitters about starting new companies. I would hate to be thought of as just a millionaire who throws his money around without any thought.

I've got an awful lot and I've done an awful lot, but the greatest treasure to me is my family and friends. My family have never asked me for a penny. Can you believe that? Not one penny. They have their own lives and they still work hard.

I like holidays, but I love home. Everyone I love is here, so it is where I want to be. Belfast and Northern Ireland are special to me and I'll never leave. I wish we could do something about the rain, but that's out of even a lottery winner's hands!

My ambition is to live long and have a lot of years to enjoy my good fortune. No point in having wealth but no health.

The freedom a lottery win provides is incredible, and I am so thankful for it. I come from a humble, working-class background and grew up in troubled times. Thanks to the lottery, I have had the best years of my life since the win.

I've been on Concorde, on cruises, stayed in the best hotels in the world. But my feet will never leave the ground ... the people of Belfast, my friends and family would never let that happen.

Top Ten Hotspots

Does where you live affect your chances of winning? The simple answer is no, but some towns and cities do enjoy a huge slice of Lottery luck. These are the top ten hotspots.

Medway Towns
Ilford
Romford
Sunderland
Newcastle-upon-Tyne
Perth
Teeside
Dartford
Hull
Bradford

The Charity Giver

In 1995, Elaine Thompson, a 38-year-old mother of two from Newcastle, won £2.75 million on her 17th wedding anniversary. She hasn't stopped since.

I felt pretty nervous as I approached the gates of Downing Street, the home of the Prime Minister and one of the most important addresses in the United Kingdom.

I was dressed for the part and had an official pass to get in, but something in the back of my mind said a girl from a terraced house in the back streets of Newcastle wouldn't be allowed past the security.

The police were polite and efficient, checked the documents and I was in. I couldn't believe they hadn't stopped me. It was fantastic. From Wallsend to Downing Street. What a journey.

I'd been lucky enough to get invited after doing fund-raising for the CLIC Sergeant Cancer Care for Children charity. I'd won £2.75

million on the lottery in 1995, but never dreamed of stopping work or taking it easy.

But it all could have been very different. We could have missed out on our big day.

We very nearly didn't do the lottery that week!

It was our 17th wedding anniversary, December 9, 1995, and my husband Derek, being cheeky, said, 'People don't normally celebrate the 17th, do they?' It had less to do with it being an odd number than with him wanting to go out for the football. Newcastle United was playing in London, and he always met up with his mates who went down for the matches.

Everything was happening in such a rush with Derek going to London that the lottery could have easily slipped through our hands. Derek normally gets the lottery tickets on a Friday or Saturday morning. In the rush to organise the football that week, he had forgotten. The last thing he said before leaving was to remind me to put the lottery on. We always put £10 on with the same set of numbers.

I know loads of people who have missed the odd week or two. Fortunately, I didn't fall into that trap.

I remember the day clearly. I spent some time with my mum and then we all watched telly in the evening. The lottery came on and I thought the numbers looked familiar. I asked my daughter Karen to fetch the ticket, but I was really relaxed. I thought we might have won a tenner. Well, she came in with the ticket and the very first line matched the numbers on the screen.

It's then that your mind goes into overdrive. Did I really put the lottery on today? Was I really in the shop earlier or am I looking at last week's ticket? I asked my daughter Karen what the date was. She said, 'Mum, it's your wedding anniversary!'

I didn't know what to do. I rang my sister-in-law but she had no idea. I phoned a friend who ran a pub, but she said she was too busy to talk. I didn't think to look at the back of the ticket. I phoned Derek's mum and she screamed and hung up. I started thinking that no one wanted to talk to me, and I still didn't know what to do. My sister-in-law eventually rang back and told me to turn the ticket over and follow the printed instructions.

It is all a bit confusing. You dream for so long about winning and what you might do with the money. Then suddenly you are right in the middle of it.

We had some neighbours round and had some tea and a bit of a gathering. Camelot were fantastic on the phone and told us exactly what would happen. Derek wasn't back yet so we couldn't celebrate properly. I'm a very level-headed Geordie, so I didn't go mad straight away.

When Derek did get back, he couldn't take it in. I knew it was £2.75 million by then, so he said he wouldn't turn the ticket over in case the numbers fell off! He was terrified the numbers would disappear or evaporate or somehow the win would slip away.

We finally all went to bed at 4 a.m., but were up two hours later because we couldn't sleep. The next day, someone from Camelot came round and the ticket was checked out. We decided to go public then because there seemed little point trying to keep it quiet. Anyway, I couldn't lie to family and friends.

We were taken to London and put up in a posh hotel where the other guests looked regal and wealthy. In trooped the Thompsons in scruffy jeans and coats. It was strange to be there knowing that we could now afford places like this.

We had room service, but I wouldn't let the kids order anything. It was £20 for a burger and chips! I didn't care how much we'd won. I wasn't paying that! Winning the jackpot doesn't wipe out your background. I was brought up to watch the pennies. £20 for a burger? You have got to be joking! We went out to find somewhere cheaper to eat.

Our first thoughts were how this fortune would affect our lives. Would the kids get bullied? Would friends take it the wrong way? How would people react? The kids, Karen and Gary, went to a good state school. We all lived on a lovely estate with good neighbours. We desperately didn't want these things to change. Neither Derek nor I are from money. We would have been horrified if people thought about us as moneybags, and judged us just because we were lottery winners.

We needn't have worried. Good friends stayed good friends and everyone accepted it. After the initial excitement, everybody just moved on.

We were already very lucky in that we had work, a nice house and two lovely kids. We were even able to take a holiday each year. We were well aware that others were on the dole, were single parents or struggling to make ends meet. We didn't want to shove the win in people's faces. It wouldn't have been right to suddenly start driving around in flashy cars. The first car we bought was a Ford Fiesta.

Again, that was our northern roots showing. We would never flash our good fortune around. We felt very lucky and very humbled to win.

We bought all the kids in the school a selection box, and all the teachers and staff champagne. When we went to the cash and carry and handed over our credit card, the guy said the company only took cash. We'd just won £2.75 million but couldn't pay. The guy thought it was hilarious that we didn't have any money on us. Derek had to go to the bank to get cash out.

We were determined to keep living normal lives. I was 38 and our children were aged 11 and five when we won. We were doing well as a family. Derek, who was 36, had a good job as a sales director and I was working as a payroll clerk. After the win, the kids stayed at the same school and Derek stayed on at work, where he had worked hard to get to the senior level.

Even though we kept things normal, the money certainly changed our lives. It gave us the ability to do things that we had only dreamed of. More importantly, we could put our kids through university.

Karen was the first member of our family to go to university. We are really proud of that. She finished her course with just £3,000 debt rather than the £20,000 that most kids have. She has now settled in Newcastle. She lives with her partner in a three-bedroom detached house with a garage, beautiful garden and only a small mortgage.

Gary will get the same benefit when he goes to university, and that makes us feel brilliant. What an achievement!

Giving your kids a great start in life is what it is all about. Like most parents, I would go without to make sure my kids have opportunities. The lottery has meant we can do that extra bit for them.

I think I appreciate everything more because of my background. I'm very close to the kids because life was never that easy when I was growing up. Derek and I are both from working-class families in Newcastle that didn't have much.

His dad was on the whalers and then in the shipyards. My dad was a chef in the Merchant Navy, but that isn't half the story. All I can say is that he had a different approach to being a parent. It was not one I was going to repeat.

My brother Ian, who was seven years older than me, saw much more of those troubled days.

Some of my memories are fairly typical of a youngster growing up. I remember my dad coming round the corner from work and Mum letting me run up the street to meet him. He would carry me back home on his shoulders.

But then it changed.

One weekend, he sent us away to a caravan site by the sea for a week. When we got home he had emptied the house. Everything was gone, and it was just a shell. He left my mum with a lot of debt and disappeared.

It was really tough for her. As a single mum in those days you couldn't get loans to buy anything, and there was a stigma about not having a husband. One of my earliest memories is of Mum going round the shops to pay off his debt at 10 shillings a week. She was liable for it all but she cleared everything, bless her. She wouldn't have the stain of bad debt on the family even though it wasn't her fault.

My dad was cruel to my mum, but she was a wonderful woman. She never had any money, but somehow she always had a hot meal for us once a day. She never moaned or passed on any bitterness. The values she instilled in us were the best gift she could have given. Her children were the most important part of her life and that never changed.

But it was still a pretty lonely life for me. Mum had to go out to work all day, and I had to let myself in when I got back from school. My brother was away in the RAF and there was no one to look after me. I had to stay in the house, so I didn't have a big circle of friends.

I was a shy and timid girl then. (No one can believe that now!) I started to bite my nails and, to this day, I can't stop.

I was really lucky to get a chance to go to a boarding school on a Government-sponsored scheme that took kids from the backstreets. I had to do loads of exams and interviews but managed to get a place at a school near Hexham. It had a farm, a swimming pool and was on the edge of a forest. It was amazing.

We went back recently to see it and Derek said, 'I didn't realise you went to school in an army camp.' It was a collection of bleak wooden huts, but to me it was paradise. It was an escape from the bad memories of home and from having no one to talk to or play with after school.

I was away for 14 weeks at a time and I loved it. I didn't really miss my mum and, at first, hated going home.

I recognised then that my childhood had its sadness, but I resolved early on not to let it bother me or hold me back.

The memories never left though. My dad was 6ft 2ins tall and my mum 4ft 11ins. When he was roughing her up one day, she poured a kettle of water on him. He left us nine times before finally staying away for good. When she found him three years later and took him to court, he could only afford to pay the equivalent of two pence a week.

My mum turned down that money. If that was all he could afford, he obviously needed it more than us, and she didn't want his money.

We built our own lives without him.

I met Derek on New Year's Eve in 1976, when he was 17 and I was 19. He had been made redundant and came to work at my firm in Newcastle.

Four years later, we were wed.

For the first six years of our marriage I earned more than him, because he was training and doing a lot of home study courses.

It was the era of the miners' strike and a

recession. Times were tough with lots of people being laid off. Newcastle was hit hard. It was distressing to see people who had worked all their lives struggling to find any jobs.

We decided to go to Aberdeen in Scotland because there were jobs in the oil industry there. We had to live in lodgings for six months before we got things sorted out. We had bought a flat in Newcastle, so we were at least on the property ladder.

In Aberdeen, we finally moved into a three-bedroom house and Karen was born.

Every now and again I thought about my father. I wanted to tell him things. I wanted him to know what a great job my mum had done, and how well we'd turned out. I thought it would be nice to walk in and say, 'Hello, Dad.' That was something I had not been able to say for 25 years.

He wasn't there to give me away when I got married. To me, that was wrong. Your father should give you away. Even though I'd moved on, his presence was still with me.

But I wouldn't look for him until my mum gave us permission. When Karen was born, Mum decided that my dad should know he had become a granddad.

I got in touch with the Salvation Army with

the last address we knew. It took them a year to find him.

We were moving from Aberdeen to Basingstoke, where Derek had got a better job. Six days before the move, we got a call to say my dad was living in Reading. That was only about 30 miles from where we were going. On the phone, they could only tell me that he had been in the Merchant Navy and had married twice.

They contacted him and arranged a meeting.

It was nerve-racking to meet him after all those years. We had agreed to meet at his work, where he was a security guard. I only had a grainy old photo of him, but I knew him as soon as I saw him. It was strange. It was nice to see him, but he was a dad in name only. There was nothing there.

After that, my mum and Ian both met him, and it was really important for them.

My mum said what she wanted to say and made friends, which made her feel a lot better. After what he'd put her through, she needed to have that chance to say how she felt. It took my brother three months to get himself together to go to see him. But then he was finally able to bury that painful past.

It was brilliant, because carrying that hate around for too long makes you a worse person. The meetings made life easier for both my mum and Ian. They finally had closure.

I didn't hate dad. I just felt disappointed that he never got in touch and didn't even know when my birthday was. I saw him once every four months, but never met his new wife or my half-brother.

As a family, we had dealt with our past, so I concentrated on bringing up my own kids. Gary had been born in 1990 and Karen was growing up quickly.

We moved into a nice house on an estate and Derek got promoted to company director. He was on a good salary with a company car and travelled all over. Three months later we won the money, which we shared with Ian.

It took me a year to tell my father. He wasn't part of my family because he had chosen his own path. I knew I didn't have to tell him, but I didn't like being dishonest about it since I had nothing to hide.

Maybe I shouldn't have told him. He was suddenly much more interested in me. He got in touch about money he needed, telling me how he was going to be evicted from his home if he didn't get his windows fixed and stuff like that. He came up with all sorts of stories. It was clear he was in touch because of the money.

I didn't feel I had a duty to look after him, especially since he hadn't looked after me. I couldn't just switch that feeling on after 26 years.

He did get a cheque but I felt it was best to make a break. You could say it was harsh but I wanted to protect my own family. I felt no strong emotion for him. All my efforts were for my own kids.

It is not something I can change. It is a chapter that has been and gone.

After two years with the money, Derek decided it was time to do something different. We had always wanted to run a holiday complex. When we were shown Champernhayes, a stunning farmhouse with cottages near Lyme Regis, in Dorset, we took the drastic decision to plunge in.

You might say we were mad, but it had always been something we wanted to do. When would we get a better chance? I felt fantastic about the challenge.

We moved down to Dorset, and I haven't heard from my dad since.

The saddest thing is that my mum passed away in 1997, when she was 70. We felt robbed of precious time with her. She was a wonderful and inspiring woman. I hope we've been able to pass on her values to our kids.

Sadly, Ian died when he was 52, so we have dealt with our fair share of tragedy. He had been playing golf with Derek when he had a fatal heart attack. His death left a huge hole in my life. I still miss him so much.

We had split the lottery win with Ian, so he had been able to give up work and enjoy life with us. We spent a great deal of time together after the win. I will always be grateful for those six years we were able to enjoy together. He helped us get Champernhayes up and running and lived with us in Dorset.

We had a massive job to do with the holiday complex. It was a little run-down, but we worked hard and even got a five-star rating. We had some great times there.

Since we lived on site, we were always on duty, so we were hardly taking it easy. We knew that we had won a great amount of money, but that it would soon disappear if we did nothing all day.

The site included a farmhouse and four cottages. Twice a year we gave free weeks to families with children suffering from cancer. The children would arrive with their wigs on and be a bit reserved. In only a couple of days they would be in and out of our house, in the pool and with the wigs off.

It was fantastic to see such happiness and very humbling to witness the kids' bravery. Karen and Gary were great with them. They were wonderful days.

But we felt we'd neglected our own kids a bit because of all the work. After six years, we sold up and took a year off. Because Ian and Grandma had died, we wanted Karen and Gary to know we were there for them. That year off was great and, again, a freedom made possible by the lottery.

People talk about the money, but it is the freedom that money buys that is the most important part of winning.

After that year off, Derek and I were ready for a new project. We spotted a restaurant on the seafront at Lyme Regis and both had the feeling we could do something with it. We made a pact that if it was still for sale in six months we would buy it. It was and we did. It was fate.

When 'By The Bay' opened, it was busy from the start. We had 52 staff to look after and that was a lot. Most of the time was brilliant, although Derek and I barely saw each other.

After five years we were still talking, so it must have worked.

We were spoilt with brilliant staff. By the Bay was always a fun place to be. We had great evenings and did lots of fund-raising there. One year we raised more than £20,000 for charity. We were really proud of that.

After five years, we decided to sell the restaurant. It was sad to move on but it was time to do something else.

Fifteen years after the win, it is time to reflect. We have had a brilliant life. We would always have done well because we worked hard and were lucky enough to have decent jobs. My start in life wasn't that great, but I met Derek and getting married to a fantastic man was a crucial turning point.

But the lottery win has given us opportunities beyond our dreams. We've been around the world, seen amazing things, met celebrities and politicians and helped other lottery winners. We live in a beautiful five-bedroom house with views over the Lyme Regis bay. Above all that, we've been able to give our kids a brilliant start in life.

I didn't have any problems with winning and I've always been a very positive person. Because of this, Camelot chose me to be an ambassador to mentor new winners and tell them what it's like to have your money worries fade away.

It was great to meet other winners and help them. There is a good community of winners who stay friends and meet at events that are often put on by Camelot.

The No. 10 visit was arranged through Camelot. I was excited beyond belief, as well as worried that they would stop an ordinary working-class girl at the gates and turn me away. I needn't have worried.

I was like a little schoolgirl, totally awestruck by No. 10. The policeman opened the door for us and we were in. It is massive, like the Tardis from Doctor Who. We walked up the main staircase where there are paintings of all the prime ministers on the walls. At the top is Margaret Thatcher looking straight down at you. There is a sense of the importance.

We were greeted by the then Prime Minister Tony Blair's wife, Cherie. She was really warm and welcoming. It felt just like she was inviting us into her house for a cosy cup of tea, rather than bringing us into the heart of power. She was very down to earth and had taken the time to find out about us. I think that says a lot about someone. It certainly put me at ease.

We met politicians and I felt like I was walking through history. It was an incredible day and I wouldn't have been there if not for the lottery. It opens doors you cannot imagine. I've been on Concorde, been to the Olympic Games, appeared on television and done all sorts of amazing things ... and it only cost £1.

The £7 Million Telephone Call

Camelot Representative - Andrew XX
Player 1 - Jane Surtees
Player 2 - Voice in background

Player 1: Oh good morning, yes, well, I've won the jackpot from last night so what do I do?

Representative: So you've got all six numbers from last night, yeah?

Player 1: Yes.

Representative: OK can you ...

Player 1: What?

Representative: Right, let me just get my pen here.

Player 1: Thank you.

Representative: I was wondering when you were going to call up today.

Player 1: Yep, here I am! Have you been waiting for this one?

Representative: The one winner from last night, yes.

Player 1:	Seven and a half million quid. I believe I'm better off?
Representative:	Yep, just over that – 7,544,200, yeah, so congratulations!
Player 1:	Thank you very much.
Representative:	Now, is it your ticket first of all?
Player 1:	It is, yes.
Representative:	Yep, brilliant, OK. Well, I need to take a few details from yourself. It'll be about five minutes. Is that OK?
Player 1:	Oh I don't know if I can afford the phone bill.
Representative:	*Laughter.* It's a local rate number.
Player 1:	*Laughter.* I'm joking.
Representative:	No problem. Right, it was the mid-week draw and it's the jackpot. Can I take your first name please?
Player 1:	Yes, it's Jane, which is just Jane. J, A, N, E.
Representative:	J, A, N, E, yeah?
Player 1:	Yep.
Representative:	Jane, yes, sorry?
Player 1:	Yes.

Representative:	Yep. And your surname please, Jane?
Player 1:	That is Surtees and it's spelt Sierra, Uniform, Romeo, Tango, Echo, Echo, Sierra.
Representative:	Thank you very much. Is that Mrs, Miss or Ms?
Player 1:	It's Mrs ... no Miss.
Representative:	OK, Jane, you're speaking to Andrew, OK?
Player 1:	Hiya.
Representative:	Right, OK, can I take your home phone number please there, Jane?
Player 1:	You can, it's XXXX XXXXXXX.
Representative:	Right, thank you very much.
Player 1:	I should be screaming down the phone. It just hasn't, I'm numb actually, it just hasn't sunk in.
Representative:	When did you find out? Was it last night or ...?
Player 1:	No, this morning! This morning, but the strange thing is me and my other half, last night, we sat there and we joked about it. You

know, what the hell would you do with 8 million quid, you know? And I said, 'Oh it's gonna be me winning it.' Didn't I, Mark? And I'm gonna win it. And ...

Representative: And you were right!

Player 1: And I came home and I did!

Representative: Women are always right.

Player 1: Yeah, I looked at Teletext and then I put it on the computer 'cause I thought, no this has gotta be a mistake. It was surreal.

Representative: You'd be surprised, I speak to a lot of winners and they're all the same. Well they're not all the same. They're all very different actually. You know some of them are quite calm. Some of them are really excited on the phone.

Player 1: Yeah.

Representative: No problem. OK, Jane, can I take your address please?

Player 1: You can, it's XXXX XXXXXXX.

Representative: Thanks so much.

Player 1:	God, I never thought I'd be doing it – at Christmas as well!
Representative:	Yeah Christmas, just in time for Christmas. *Laughter.*
Player 1:	If you're gonna win any jackpot it's gotta be a rollover and this one is the one I've been waiting for, eh?
Representative:	Exactly, good things happen to people who wait. So can you read me out your respective numbers on your ticket there please, Jane?
Player 1:	I can, it's 9, 11, 23, 27, 29 and 33, had them since day one!
Representative:	Really?
Player 1:	Yes.
Representative:	Any big prizes?
Player 1:	No, I've never won. I've never won more than a tenner. And we've stuck with them. I've been to a lot of places and I always, I'd always say to my fella, 'Oh God, I've gotta get my lottery! I've gotta get the … you know, gotta get back 'cause one of these days …'

Representative:	Right. And are you part of a syndicate at all or is it all yours?
Player 1:	No, no, it's mine. It's my own private card.
Representative:	OK.
Player 1:	Card? Oh God, I can't speak now. There it goes, the madness is setting in. It's my own ticket.
Representative:	OK, no problem. Right, which line have you won on? Line A, B, C?
Player 1:	I've won on B.
Representative:	B. OK. And where did you buy your ticket from? Do you remember?
Player 1:	Oh dear me ... it could have been the sp... I think it might have been the Spar shop in Whitby.
Representative:	OK. So the time is 9:11, OK, have you put your name and address on the back of the ticket yet?
Player 1:	No not yet. I daren't touch the damn thing! Yeah!
Representative:	No probs. If I can just ask you

	to put your name and address on the back of the ticket while I'm on the phone and also, get a separate piece of paper as well please, Jane.
Player 1:	Oh I think we're gonna have a good Christmas! Oh my God, my pen isn't working! I can't afford a pen! Oh, help!
Player 2:	I've got one in the van ...
Player 1:	I've got one in ... can you just bear with me one sec?
Representative:	That's OK. I'll wait here.
Player 1:	Just stay there, I won't be a ... I'm back. So I put my name on it, yeah?
Representative:	Yes, please, yeah.
Player 1:	*Inaudible.* God, I've not had any sleep, I didn't go to bed till about half past three so ...
Representative:	Oh right.
Player 1:	*Inaudible.* Yep.
Representative:	Excellent. Have you told anyone else about your win yet?
Player 1:	My, my mum was here ...
Representative:	Your mum, yeah?
Player 1:	And she, I believe she, she's

	called my brother and that's it.
Representative:	OK.
Player 1:	And my partner.
Representative:	OK.
Player 1:	He's the first person I told. *Background voices.* Oh shut up you! Yes and no. Yes but no but, if you know what I mean?
Representative:	Yeah, no problem, just to advise you, Jane, it's probably best not to discuss the win until you are advised to do so by Camelot, OK? I'm going to give you my name, it's Andrew.
Player 1:	Good morning, Andrew!
Representative:	OK, the reason why I'm giving you my name is when someone calls you back they'll say they're giving you a call in regards to the conversation you've had with myself.
Player 1:	Yep.
Representative:	OK, they won't mention they're calling from the

lottery or Camelot at all. OK?
This is for security reasons.

Player 1:   Yeah sure.

Representative: OK. You say it's best to give
                    you a call back on your
                    mobile. Is that correct?

Player 1:   Yep, try my mobile, it'll be
                    fine. I am trying to remember
                    if I left my charger in my
                    hotel last night. Sorry, yeah,
                    I think I can afford a
                    new charger. Sorry yes, so
                    what, what happens now?
                    Do I have to come to ...?
                    Where is the nearest
                    Camelot office to Whitby
                    then?

Representative: Right, Whitby. You're in the
                    middle of ... some places I'm
                    afraid. They're quite far away
                    ... I'm sorry. Aintree in
                    Liverpool is probably your
                    nearest office.

Player 1:   Yeah, so ... when will it be?

Representative: Yeah, basically, what they do
                    is a winner's advisor will give
                    you a call back to arrange a
                    date and time when it's

	convenient for you to come along.
Player 1:	That could be today!
Representative:	I mean, if they've got an appointment today then you know, it's no problem, they can book you in and you can come in and collect your cheque. You will go through the whole winners' experience.
Player 1:	Yeah ... we're off tomorrow though, aren't we, Mark? We've got, we could maybe do it tomorrow ... they'll tell us, won't they, yeah.
Representative:	Yeah, they'll tell you when they've got appointments available, OK. So they'll give you a call on your mobile and speak to you about what you need to bring with you.
Player 1:	Yep.
Representative:	OK, do you have any questions at all?
Player 1:	No, no, it's real, isn't it? There's no doubt about it? I've won it, haven't I?

Representative:	Sorry? Well, until your ticket is actually scanned on one of our lottery machines in the centre I can't confirm.
Player 1:	Yeah.
Representative:	As with all prizes, even if it's £10, you know, until you actually have the ticket scanned on a machine it's a claim.
Player 1:	There's no doubt though, there's only one winner, isn't there?
Representative:	Well, the numbers you've given me are the winning numbers and there's only one winner from last night.
Player 1:	And it was a rollover?
Representative:	Which is you.
Player 1:	And it is me! Ha, yes!
Representative:	Luckiest person in the country today!
Player 1:	Oh, I am the luckiest person in the country today! And do you know what as well? I'm really nice as well! Which is even better. That helps, doesn't it?

Representative:	You what, sorry?
Player 1:	I said I'm really nice as well which is even better. *Laughter*.
Representative:	*Laughter*.
Player 1:	Yeah, I'm a just cause!
Representative:	Yep.
Player 1:	A lot of people will benefit from this I can tell you.
Representative:	You seem very down to earth and everything.
Player 1:	Absolutely! Can't get much more down to earth.
Representative:	Keep your feet on the ground and you'll be fine.
Player 1:	Yep, I'm actually gonna start living it large now, when I put down the phone.
Representative:	I wouldn't blame you.
Player 1:	Well, how soon will it be before I get the call?
Representative:	Well, it shouldn't be too long. One of the winners' advisors will give you a call back and because you are the only jackpot winner from last night you'll get preferential treatment.

Player 1:	Great. Just double check my two phone numbers, will you?
Representative:	Yes, of course, yeah. Mobile number is XXXXXXXXXXX.
Player 1:	Yep.
Representative:	And the home number is XXXXXXXXXXX.
Player 1:	That's it, you've got it.
Representative:	OK.
Player 1:	Right, what the hell do I do with this ticket for goodness sake?
Representative:	Keep it somewhere safe, yeah?
Player 1:	Yep.
Representative:	I am here until 5.30 p.m. today so if you have any questions at all there, Jane, give me a call.
Player 1:	Yep.
Representative:	So if you've got any queries at all.
Player 1:	Yep.
Representative:	Just speak to myself.
Player 1:	OK, Andrew, I will do. I'm gonna go and have a cup of tea now.

Representative:	You and your family enjoy the win though.
Player 1:	We will, believe you me, we really will, yep. OK, thank you then.
Representative:	No trouble.
Player 1:	Very nice to talk to you.
Representative:	Many thanks now.
Player 1:	Yep, speak to somebody soon then. Cheers.
Representative:	Cheers, bye.
Player 1:	Bye, bye.
Representative:	Bye.

The Lottery's Legacy

The National Lottery marked its 15th Anniversary in November 2009. That's 15 years in which National Lottery grants to projects in the arts, sport, heritage, health, education, environment, charity and voluntary sectors have made a huge difference to people and communities across the UK.

More than £23 billion has been raised for the Good Causes by lottery players since The National Lottery began in November 1994, and over 335,000 grants have been made to projects across the UK.

Every week players raise around £25 million for Good Causes. That breaks down to more than £3.5 million per day and an incredible £148,000 per hour, or £2,480 per minute that has helped and is helping to change the face of the UK.

The grants range from small, local awards to multi-million-pound schemes of national importance that have touched every corner of the UK:

- More than 500 public parks have been given a face lift with £500 million of Lottery money.
- More than £1 billion has been raised for projects that support health and well-being.
- Land equal in size to more than 100,000 football pitches has been bought for nature conservation.
- More than £1.3 billion of Lottery funding has been awarded to museums and galleries across the UK.
- £10 billion has been invested in projects that benefit children and young people.
- 436 Olympic and Paralympic medals have been won by Lottery-funded athletes, with Beijing 2008 being Team GB's best medal haul for 100 years.

The National Lottery will contribute up to £2.2 billion to the building of the support structure for the London Olympics in 2012 and its legacy.

Wherever you are in the UK, it's more than likely that lottery funding has improved your local area in some way. The variety of the projects that the lottery has helped to make happen is truly astounding.

And for those lucky winners, the freedom and security that money buys is their greatest prize. Whether they spend their fortune on university for the kids, business investments for charity or boob jobs for sisters, these people become fairy godmothers granting wishes to the people they care about.

Never have a small piece of paper and some numbers on a screen been worth so much.

Quick Reads

Books in the Quick Reads series

Quick Reads

Short, sharp shots of entertainment

As fast and furious as an action film. As thrilling as a theme park ride. Quick Reads are short sharp shots of entertainment — brilliantly written books by bestselling authors and celebrities. Whether you're an avid reader who wants a quick fix or haven't picked up a book since school, sit back, relax and let Quick Reads inspire you.

We would like to thank all our partners in the Quick Reads project for their help and support:

Arts Council England
The Department for Business, Innovation and Skills
NIACE
unionlearn
National Book Tokens
The Reading Agency
National Literacy Trust
Welsh Books Council
Basic Skills Cymru, Welsh Assembly Government
The Big Plus Scotland
DELNI
NALA

Quick Reads would also like to thank the Department for Business, Innovation and Skills; Arts Council England and World Book Day for their sponsorship and NIACE for their outreach work.

Quick Reads is a World Book Day initiative.
www.quickreads.org.uk   www.worldbookday.com

Other resources

Free courses are available for anyone who wants to develop their skills. You can attend the courses in your local area. If you'd like to find out more, phone 0800 66 0800.

Don't get by get on 0800 66 0800

A list of books for new readers can be found on www.firstchoicebooks.org.uk or at your local library.

read
readingagency.org.uk

Publishers Barrington Stoke (www.barringtonstoke.co.uk) and New Island (www.newisland.ie) also provide books for new readers.

Barrington Stoke

OPEN DOOR

The BBC runs an adult basic skills campaign. See www.bbc.co.uk/raw.

BBC
raw
skills for everyday life

www.quickreads.org.uk   www.worldbookday.com

About the Author

Danny Buckland is a writer and journalist who has followed the Lottery since it started in 1994.

He has interviewed jackpot winners and shared their hopes and fears as they get used to being millionaires.

Danny has worked for many national newspapers including The Sun, The Daily Mail and the Sunday Express.

He is married with two children and lives in London.